W9-BBS-518

The Publishers wish to thank Estancia Santa Susana for the photographs of the Pampas, to Mister Carlos María Bazán for those of pato and polo, to Mister Gregorio Plotnicki from the Mano Blanca Museum, to Mister Nicolás Rubió for the photographs on filete and to Miss Nina Passone for the aereal view of 9 de Julio Avenue.

Design and photography: Sophie le Comte
© Maizal Ediciones, 2005
Las reproducciones están condicionadas al fin exclusivamente didáctico y orientativo de esta obra (art. 10, Ley 11.723)
Hecho el depósito que previene la ley 11.723
ISBN 987-9479-23-8
Published by Maizal
Muñiz 438, B1640FDB, Martínez, Buenos Aires, Argentina
E–mail: info@maizal.com
All rights reserved. No part of this publication may be transmitted or reproduced in any form, or by any means, electronic or mechanical, including photocopy, recording, or any storage and retrieval system, without the prior permission in writing from the publisher.
Printed in November 2005 by Morgan Internacional.

Buenos Aires

MAIZAL
EDICIONES

INTRODUCTION

Buenos Aires was founded for the first time by Don Pedro de Mendoza, who arrived with a huge fleet from Spain in 1536. The first foundation survived only for a short time, because it was constantly harassed by Indian tribes that put fire to the poor settlement. Eventually, its starving population abandoned Buenos Aires and fled to Asunción del Paraguay.

The second founder of Buenos Aires was Juan de Garay, who founded the city coming from Asunción, in 1580.

As there were neither stones nor wood in the region where the city was founded, the first houses were built of adobe, a mass of earth dried in the sun. These houses did not last for a long time, and no building of that period remains.

The city was built in accordance to the *Leyes de Indias*, Indies' laws, a body of laws passed by the Spanish King which demanded that a newly founded city had to be divided into blocks as if the city were a checkerboard and the surrounding plots of land had to be given to those who accompanied the founder of the city in his enterprise.

In 1776 Buenos Aires became the residence of the Government of the Viceroyalty of the Río de la Plata, and its port grew in importance.

English troops invaded Buenos Aires in 1806 y 1807. In both attacks, the English were defeated. Napoleonic invasions in Spain and the certainty that the people in Buenos Aires were able to defend themselves against any possible invasion, led the *criollos*, the people born in the colonies, to believe that it might be possible to think of Independence. On the 25 May 1810, they started this movement by appointing the first native government. Independence was eventually declared on 9 July, 1816.

Many years passed and neither the people in Buenos Aires nor the people in the rest of the country could come to a compromise as regarding the status of the City of Buenos Aires and the form of government of the country, until finally in 1880, Buenos Aires, among other cities, was chosen to be the capital city of the country.

In 1871 a terrible yellow–fever epidemic forced the people to move to the northern part of the city, and leave the basin of the Riachuelo which was thought to be the source of contamination. The Riachuelo is a small river that marks the limit of the city in the South. Today the neighbourhood of La Boca is on the Riachuelo.

By the end of the nineteenth century, a large–scale immigration settled down, and the population of Buenos Aires grew rapidly.

Today, the federal district of Buenos Aires is 200 square kilometres in extent and has a population of 3.000.000 inhabitants. Greater Buenos Aires, the federal district together with the surrounding towns, has a population of 9.000.000 inhabitants.

SKYLINE OF BUENOS AIRES

The skyline of Buenos Aires is best seen from the river, either from a boat or from the Ecological Reserve.
Eduardo Mallea, an important Argentine writer called Buenos Aires "The City on the Immobile River".

Buenos Aires in the first half of the eighteenth century.

Costanera Sur

The Costanera Sur, the Southern Riverside Path used to be an elegant promenade that ran along the Río de la Plata. It was, for many years, a sort of seaside resort for the porteños. Between the breakwater (today the entrance to the Ecological Reserve) and the round pergola, there were stairs that went down to the water. This resort is no longer by the water but one can walk up and down the four big avenues: Intendente Noel, De los Italianos, Dr. Tristán Achával Rodríguez and España and admire the immense river and the statues along them, which are among the best in the city.

Nereids' Fountain.
Lola Mora, the first woman sculptor in Argentina, made this fountain in Rome in 1902. Made of Carrara marble, it has been placed in the Costanera, in front of the river.

Ecological Reserve.
The reserve is made up of 380 blocks. This
landfill area has a natural microclimate similar
to the one found by the first settlers in the
sixteenth century.

10

Puerto Madero

The construction of this port began in 1880 on a plot of 170 hectares. It has four closed interconnected docks that run parallel to the river, and 16 buildings which were used for storing cargo. They were designed by the English engineer John Hawkshaw. Puerto Madero stayed abandoned for many years, but in the nineties restoration was begun. Today it is a seafront promenade with very modern apartment houses, office buildings, excellent restaurants, cinemas, drugstores, hotels, museums, a university, etc. Puerto Madero, a link between the river and the city, is Buenos Aires' most modern neighbourhood.

12

Buenos Aires, J. Dulín (1839–1919)

*Women's bridge.
This pedestrian bridge was designed by the famous Spanish architect Santiago Calatrava. This is his first bridge in South America.*

Hilton Hotel in Puerto Madero. This modern hotel was designed by Mario Roberto Álvarez.

Fragata Sarmiento.
Built in 1898 in England, was up to 1961 a training ship of the
Naval School.

Puerto Madero from the water.
At the back, the neighbourhood of Catalinas. (p. 15)

La Boca

The history of La Boca, the most colourful neighbourhood of the city, started with the history of the first foundation of Buenos Aires. The boca, the mouth of the Riachuelo (meaning: a small river) was the only safe shelter where the ships of the imposing fleet of the Adelantado Don Pedro de Mendoza, could be left anchored. An *adelantado* was the governor of a border province under Spanish colonial rule. At that time, the basin of the Riachuelo was in the hands of the querandíes, a nomadic tribe of native Indians who used to fish on the riverside of this marshy zone.

Football is the national passion. Boca Juniors is one of the most famous football clubs in the world.

Caminito is a hundred meter long pedestrian street where one can admire sculptures, murals, etc. made by La Boca artists. There are also spontaneous street shows: singers, tango dancers, mimes, etc.

The Riachuelo was the reason why the first settlers chose this site to build the city. This small river slowly meanders on a flat plain to enter the Río de la Plata in a coast made of hard rock. The old bridge built in 1914 was constructed to link both banks of the Riachuelo and was closed down in 1960. The mobile platform could carry cars and even tramways. The metalwork was prepared in England and as pre fabricated pieces crossed the Atlantic Ocean. It is 8 metres wide and 12 metres long.

Caminito used to be a railway branch line, that is the reason why the houses have no doors to the street, and only windows and balconies overlook Caminito.
It is called Caminito after Juan de Dios Filiberto´s most famous tango.

Thanks to modern constructions and dikes, flooding, feared by the people living in La Boca, has ceased to be a problem.

In the eighteenth century, the neighbourhood started growing. Yards to store cargo to be sold at the port of La Boca were built: shipyards, salteries, wool and charcoal warehouses, tanneries, timber yards. The neighbourhood was peopled by sailors and shipyard workers.

When in 1890 the large scale immigration to Argentina started, and Italians, especially those coming from Genoa, settled near La Boca, the neighbourhood grew rapidly. The zone was seething with people, work and life. The *xeneizes* (people from Genoa) devoted themselves mainly to naval occupations: they were boat–builders, caulkers, sail masters, figurehead carvers. Many had brought socialistic views from home; some of them were even anarchists.

They were simple men, hard working and sensitive people who helped with their efforts to the development of Argentina's progress.

Proa Foundation. The office of this foundation is a building constructed in 1880, with an Italian neoclassical façade. Today this foundation is one of the meeting points of social and artistic activities in Buenos Aires.

Benito Quinquela Martín's Museum.

Magallanes Street. This street is famous for its art galleries and painters' ateliers.

20

Tango in Caminito.

Not all of the people who settled in La Boca were Italians; there were also Turks, Greeks, Dalmatians and other peoples from the Mediterranean.

The first houses made of wood and corrugated iron were built on wooden piles to avoid flooding, and painted in brilliant and intense colours. They were interesting examples of architecture without architects with spontaneous solutions dictated by necessity. These strident colours of marine varnish leftovers turned to be a distinctive characteristic of La Boca. This feature was supported by Benito Quinquela Martín, La Boca' most famous painter. Apart from corrugated iron houses, there are in La Boca many houses from the end of the nineteenth century which have Italian façades.

La Boca was from the very beginning, the place of inspiration for many painters. The most famous of them all was precisely Benito Quinquela Martín (1890–1977). He was La Boca's greatest benefactor. His artistic success was always accompanied by countless donations for his beloved neighbourhood. The Museum, his house–workshop, the Teatro de la Ribera were some of the thankful painter's presents. The Museum shows an ample view of Argentine art of the first half of the twentieth century. There is a very interesting show of figureheads in this museum as well.

San Juan Evangelista Church was inaugurated in 1886. The plot of land was a present of an English soldier who had arrived during the first English invasion and, as several other English soldiers, stayed in Buenos Aires for good.

23

Alfredo Lazzari (1871–1949).
This Italian artist was the teacher of many
important painters of La Boca as for instance
Fortunato Lacámera and Benito Quinquela
Martín.

Benito Quinquela Martín (1890–1977).
His pictures are about the workers of La Boca,
the ships, the Vuelta de Rocha, the factories.
His colours reflect the lively colour of his
neighbourhood.

La Vuelta de Rocha.
In the Plazoleta de los Suspiros, the Sighs Square, the immigrants used to meet to talk about their
far away homeland. This used to be the port for the loaded barges that carried the cargo to the ships
anchored in the outer port.
It was here that Admiral Guillermo Brown (1777–1857) armed his fleet during the wars of Independence.
Today, the Vuelta de Rocha is the hub of all artistic movements of the neighbourhood.

SAN TELMO

San Telmo and Montserrat lie to the south of the Plaza de Mayo. Many descendants of the founders of Buenos Aires lived in these neighbourhoods until 1871, when a very severe yellow fever epidemic forced them to migrate to the northern neighbourhoods. The big houses they left behind were soon occupied by immigrants and were turned into *conventillos*. A *conventillo* used to be a big, long house with rooms that opened onto a common patio where many families lived. They usually lacked hygiene and privacy. Most of those houses have disappeared; there are just a few left in San Telmo.

This is the narrowest house in Buenos Aires. It is on San Lorenzo Street in San Telmo.

"San Francisco Church" C. Pellegrini, (1800–1875).

San Pedro Telmo.

Santo Domingo.

San Ignacio.

Four of the most beautiful churches in town are in San Telmo: San Pedro Telmo, Santo Domingo, San Ignacio and San Francisco with the adjacent chapel called San Roque.
San Ignacio is the oldest building in town; its construction was started in 1670. The Jesuits already used bricks for this building.

San Francisco.

San Roque Chapel.

The district is called after the church, dedicated to Saint Pedro Telmo. He is the patron saint of sailors that is why he is always represented with a small ship in his arms.

San Ignacio, the oldest church in Buenos Aires is in the so called *Manzana de las Luces*, the Square of the Enlightenment. Buenos Aires' intelligentsia studied here. The most famous school, the Colegio Nacional de Buenos Aires, is in this block and so was the former Jesuit school.

In the towers of Santo Domingo church one can still see the shrapnel holes that were fired during the English Invasions in the first years of the nineteenth century.

This neighbourhood is crossed by several tunnels, which were built in colonial times. They were probably built by the Jesuits, who used to communicate underground, from one church to the other. The English invaders reported that when they were fighting, they did not understand how soldiers, that they had seen in front of them, after a very short time, they turned up again, but behind them.

Square of the Enlightenment.

The San Telmo neighbourhood is packed with antiques shops, art galleries, bars and places to dance tango. Every Sunday, one can visit the Antiques' Fair in Dorrego Square. It is full of tango dancers, mimes, living statues and singers.

This old building houses a famous restaurant called El Viejo Almacén. It is in one of the few corners of Buenos Aires that has no chamfered corner.

33

"Carlos Gardel" filete by León Untroib.

Tango, a national passion is danced in the streets of Buenos Aires.

The houses on the street Jean Jaures and other streets near by, have been painted following the tradition of the filete. Filete is a special ornamentation used to decorate carts and trucks. As many South American products, it developed as a mixture of several styles: the style of the French typographers, the decorations of buildings made by Spanish and Italian architects, and a lot of originality added by those who painted the filete. Today the filete is used to decorate just anything and it has become a distinctive feature of Buenos Aires. (Photograph, Nicolás Rubió).

Central Market

The Central Market, the Mercado de Abasto, which was constructed in 1929, has five long naves, the highest of which is twenty metres high. This market, which has recently been refurbished as mall, was for many years the principal foodstuffs market in Buenos Aires.

Because of the kind of people that lived around the market, this neighbourhood was the perfect site for the tango to develop. Carlos Gardel, the famous tango interpreter, lived in Abasto.

Parque Lezama

It is said that Parque Lezama was the place chosen to found the city. The Río de la Plata reached Parque Lezama at that time.

This beautiful park was the garden of a very rich merchant from Salta, a province in northern Argentina, called José G. Lezama. What used to be his house, a very big building in Italian style, is today the National History Museum. There, one can see objects related to Argentine history, up to 1950. There are arms, coins, pictures, uniforms, furniture and documents.

In the park there are monuments, historic buildings, an amphitheatre used in summertime, a small temple, called Lovers' Temple, a fountains and a big terrace.

There is a bust representing the German soldier Ulrich Schmidl, who wrote the first history of the city. There is also fountain called Neptune and the Naiads, a big monument to the first founder of Buenos Aires: Don Pedro de Mendoza, a Galician *Cruceiro*, a small place with statues of Palas Athena and *La Romana*.

In front of the park, one can visit the Russian Orthodox Church, called Holy Trinity; it has five onion–form domes which have been decorated with mosaics.

Plaza de Mayo

Plaza de Mayo is Buenos Aires' most important square. It has been, and still is, the scenery for everything that has been important in the history of the country. In front of the Casa Rosada, the Pink House, is the old Town hall, called Cabildo and the Municipality that houses the Government of the federal district of the city.

The Cabildo used to be the seat of the Spanish government in colonial times. There is not much left of the beautiful building one can admire in old prints. Most of the building has been rebuilt in 1940, copying those prints, but it was shortened to leave room for the two avenues at the sides, Avenida de Mayo and Diagonal Sur.

In the Cabildo there is a historical museum which can be visited. Behind the Cabildo, there is a clock tower which used to belong to the seat of the government of the city.

Avenida de Mayo.
The Avenida de Mayo was the first boulevard in Buenos Aires and was designed after the French architect Hausmann, when Buenos Aires dreamt of being Paris in South America. It was built in the second half of the nineteenth century, when Buenos Aires started to grow rapidly.

40

Plaza de Mayo. Pink House and May Pyramid.

The Casa Rosada, seat of the National Government, is placed between two big squares, the Plaza Colón and the Plaza de Mayo.

The Plaza Colón has the circular form of the old Customs House of Buenos Aires, called Taylor's Customs House. The statue of Colón was a present of the Italian residents to the city of Buenos Aires in 1810. The big building at one of the sides of the square, the Edificio Libertador, is the seat of the Commander in Chief of the Army.

In front of the Casa Rosada, on the Plaza de Mayo there is a monument to Manuel Belgrano. Belgrano was the creator of the Argentine flag.

"Fort of Buenos Aires", C. Pellegrini, (1800–1875). The Pink House was built on this plot of land.

Colón Square. *(p. 42)*   *Pink House.*

44

"Cabildo", Albérico Isola (1827–1850).
This is how the original Cabildo looked like. Under these arcades the neighbours used to meet and the balcony was used to make announcements by colonial authorities.

The Cabildo is probably the most important non religious building in Buenos Aires. As in all Spanish towns, it was built in front of the main square, which was called Plaza Mayor at that time.

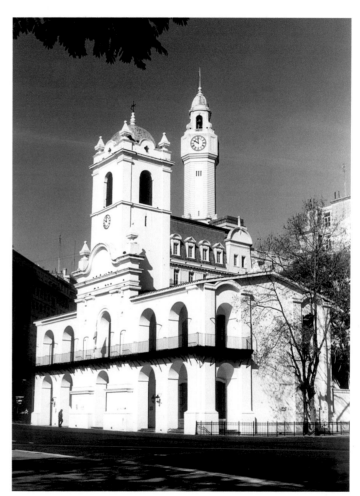

Cabildo.

Arcades of the Cabildo.

Cathedral of Buenos Aires.

At one of the sides of the square, there is the Catedral Metropolitana, the Cathedral. Its façade is in neoclassic style. The scene in the tympanum represents the meeting of Joseph and his father and symbolizes the meeting of all Argentines that had been quarrelling for a long time.

The City, the bank district of Buenos Aires lies to the north of the Cathedral. This district is full of life during workdays, but is empty at night and during weekends.

General San Martin's Mausoleum.
In a lateral chapel to the right, the Grenadiers guard San Martin's Mausoleum in the Cathedral. In odd number hours, one can see Grenadiers changing guards.

47

Detail of the floor of the Cathedral.

"View of Buenos Aires in 1845" Rudolf Carlsen (1812–1892).

Concejo Deliberante.
This tower of the municipal council has a
carillon of thirty bells built in 1932. The façade is
crowned by 26 sculptures by Argentine artists.

"May Pyramid", photograph taken in 1880.

At the corner of Rivadavia and Reconquista Streets is the National Bank of Argentina built by architect Alejandro Bustillo, inaugurated in 1952. Inside, there is an immense 30 metre high dome.

Juan de Garay, founder of Buenos Aires. Sculpture by G. H. Eberlein (1847–1926).

51

Central Post Office.
This building, built in 1928, was designed
by Roberto Maillart.

Avenida de Mayo

The Avenida de Mayo, an avenue that links Plaza de Mayo with the Plaza de los Dos Congresos, is Buenos Aires' first boulevard and it was designed after the style of the boulevards in Paris. In 1913, under the Avenida de Mayo, the first underground in Latin America was constructed.

All along the Avenida de Mayo, there are many very famous, old cafés: the Tortoni, founded in 1858, is the most famous of them all. It is one of the musts in Buenos Aires.

Many of the buildings on the Avenida de Mayo have very beautiful domes and turrets. Those on the buildings of Avenida de Mayo and San José, La Inmobiliaria, the Pasaje Barolo, etc, are worth seeing.

Old Postcard of Avenida de Mayo.

Corner of the Streets San Martín and Rivadavia.

The dome of the Congreso reflected on a building.

Domes of the Avenida de Mayo.

Congress.

The Parliament building, that houses both legislative cameras, called Congreso, is in Greco–Roman classical style. It was designed by the Italian architect Victor Meano between 1896 and 1906. Its dome is 85 m high and has a beautiful lantern at the top. The triumphal quadriga placed on the peristyle of the entrance, was sculptured by Víctor de Pol, a famous Venetian artist.

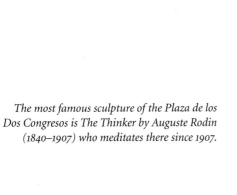

The most famous sculpture of the Plaza de los Dos Congresos is The Thinker by Auguste Rodin (1840–1907) who meditates there since 1907.

THE PORTEÑO

The inhabitant of Buenos Aires is called *porteño*, because Buenos Aires is *the* port of the country. He is well educated, arrogant, melancholic and extremely sensitive.

He has a passion for talking and one can see him in endless debates, arguing about just anything, while sipping a cup of coffee. Three topics dominate his conversation: sports, especially football; politics, and the current situation.

He has a near religious attitude as regards friendship. He likes to see and be seen, and will always have a flattering comment ready when a beautiful girl passes by. And the porteña, the woman of Buenos Aires, is usually meticulously groomed, even when she just goes shopping.

The porteño loves to stay up late, so bars, places to eat pizza, restaurants and even several bookshops, are open well after midnight and the discotheques get packed at two o'clock in the morning.

Lunfardo is the slang of Buenos Aires which includes many words introduced by immigrants and, although it started as the language of the lower classes, today it is used by almost everybody. One of the striking characteristics is the changing of the syllabic order of words. You may hear *feca* for café, *jermu* for mujer (woman), *rioba* for barrio (neighbourhood).

To go shopping is also a passion, even if nothing is bought. The porteño likes to stroll up and down the streets with nice shops or to go to a shopping centre and spend the whole afternoon window shopping. When tired, he will just sit in a café and have a cup of coffee.

The other passion is the cinema or the theatre. And then after the performance, there is usually a restaurant waiting for the porteño.

The ceiling of Galerias Pacífico was painted by famous Southamerican painters.

Café Tortoni.
Journalists, bohemians, famous visitors have visited this old café: the King of Spain, José Ortega y Gasset, Miguel de Unamuno, Rubén Darío, Amado Nervo, Alfonsina Storni, Vittorio Gassman, Hilary Clinton, Miguel de Molina, Lilly Pons, Josephine Baker.

The café is the usual meeting point where porteños argue about politics, about economy, meet friends, a place for students and solitary people. Enrique Santos Discépolo in a tango says that the bar is the school where one learns about philosophy, dice, and cruel poetry.

Café Tortoni.

63

Downtown

The streets Avenida de Mayo, Callao, Santa Fe and Alem form a rectangle that encircles the centre of Buenos Aires. This district, together with Catalinas, Puerto Madero and Once are the neighbourhoods where the political, administrative, cultural, economic and commercial activities are carried on. Not only those for Buenos Aires but for the whole country as well.

Many buildings have been demolished to make place for new ones: the Church of San Nicolás de Bari was built in the site where today stands the Obelisk, and the neighbourhood is still called San Nicolás, although the church is no longer there. From one of the towers of that old church, the national flag was hoisted for the first time in Buenos Aires.

Where the armaments factory and the artillery station used to be, today the Court House stands; and Plaza Lavalle and the Teatro Colón (which was build during the first years of the twentieth century) were built where a railway station used to be.

9 de Julio Avenue is 140 metres wide and it is reputed to be the widest street in the world.

9 de Julio Avenue.

In the crossing of 9 de Julio Avenue and Corrientes Avenue, the Obelisk, the symbol of Buenos Aires, was erected in 1936. It was constructed by architect Alberto Prebisch to commemorate the four hundredth anniversary of the first foundation of Buenos Aires. It is 67,5 metres high and was built in 60 days. In September in the 9 de Julio Avenue, one can admire the beautiful lapachos *(Tabebuia Avellanedae)*, in November, the blue jacarandas *(Jacaranda mimosifolia)* and in February the pink and white palos borrachos *(Chorisia insignis)*.

Since this fountain has been moved several times, it is called the "Travelling Fountain".

April 1936, the Obelisk is being built.

The Teatro Colón was inaugurated in 1908, it is one of the biggest opera houses in the world. It seats 2487 spectators and its big auditorium is 75 metres long.

The façade of the Teatro Cervantes, designed by Fernando Aranda and Bartolomé Repetto, was ornamented imitating the plateresque style of the University of Alcalá de Henares in Spain.

*The Grand Synagogue on Liber-
tad Street is the most important
synagogue in the city. It was designed by the architects Alejandro
Enquin and Eugenio Gantner.*

Florida street used to be the street that linked the centre of Buenos Aires with the bullring, which used to be in what today is Plaza San Martín. This street was the first one to have cobblet paving and from the twentieth century on, it is a commercial street. There were and are many important buildings on Florida Street: the Jockey Club, the most elegant club in Buenos Aires, which was burnt down in 1955, used to be there; the building of the Centro Naval which is a good example of French Academy style has a magnificent entrance; the Güemes Mall with its tango shows; El Ateneo bookshop; The Pacífico Mall.

First seat of the Jockey Club on Florida street.

The City is the name given to the district where all important banks and other financial enterprises have been built around the Commodities Exchange. This old building, designed by the architect Alejandro Christophersen, was built in 1916.

The Central Bank was designed in 1876 by the architects Hunt and Schroeder. The architect of the National Bank was achitect Bustillo and it was built in 1937. To the right, the Bank of Boston, built in 1924 by Chambers & Thomas. The former Bank of London was designed by the architects Testa, Sánchez Elía, Peralta Ramos y Agostini.

The Gran Rex cinema was designed by Alberto Prebisch. It was built in 1937.

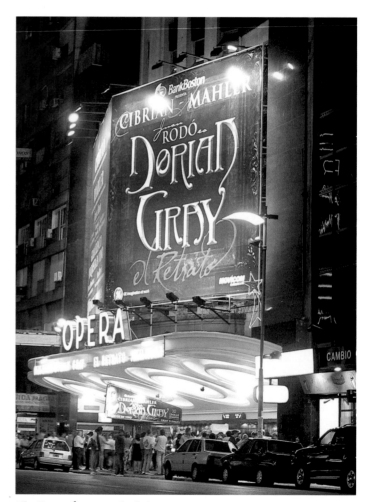

The Teatro Ópera was built in 1935.

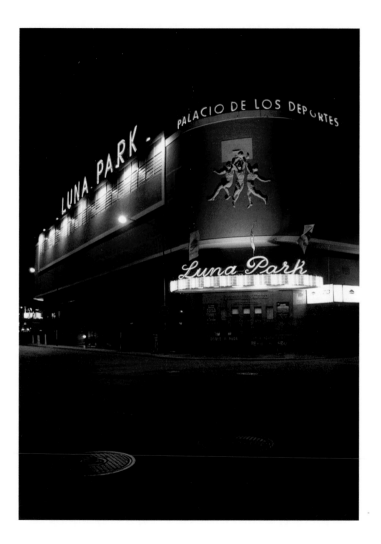

Porteños call Corrientes Avenue "the street that never sleeps". Mentioned in many tangos, along this avenue one will find many cinemas, theatres, restaurants and bookshops. This seventy block long street starts in the neighbourhood of Chacarita and ends near the river, where the Correo Central (the Central Post Office) and the Luna Park have been built.

The crossing of Florida Street and Corrientes Avenue is packed during midday on working days.

Luna Park.
The Luna Park was built to house sport events, especially boxing matches. Since it can sit 15000 spectators, it is also used for artistic shows and political meetings.

Catalinas

The Sheraton Hotel was built in front of Retiro Railway Station by the architects Sánchez Elía, Peralta Ramos and Agostini in 1972. Behind the Sheraton Hotel is the district called Catalinas, with its big buildings that house the headquarters of many important enterprises. The name was taken from a convent nearby.

Sheraton Hotel.

República Building, designed by architect César Pelli.

RETIRO

Retiro is the name given to the district around Retiro Railway Station. The name derives from a chapel which had been built in the eighteenth century. Then the name was used by the wealthy Agustín de Robles, who called his house, built in 1691, El Retiro.

This same house was then used by two big English and French slaves' companies during the eighteenth century.

*Retiro Railway Station was designed by the English architects Eustace Conder, Roger Conder, Frances Farmer and Sydney Follet in 1915.
The prefabricated iron pieces used for its construction were brought from England.*

The English Tower has been placed in front of the station. It was designed by Ambrose Poynter and was a present of the English residents in Buenos Aires in 1910. It is more than 60 metres high and the clocks started working in 1916, and have not stopped ever since. The faces are 4 metres in diameter and are made of English opaline.

This watercolour painted in 1829 by E.E. Vidal reproduces the site where today is Plaza San Martín.

The site of Plaza San Martín was occupied by a bullring that had been inaugurated in 1801. It was an octagonal construction in Moorish style which was big enough to hold ten thousand spectators. In 1807, the native army shot from the windows of the bullring against the English invaders. That is why it was from then on called Field of Glory. General José de San Martín trained the Grenadier's Regiment in this square, so it was also called Mars Field.

At the end of the nineteenth century, Charles Thays designed the new square. He was the park designer who brought the beautiful lapachos, magnolias and the giant ficus to Buenos Aires.

The traditional families, who had lived in the southern part of the city before the yellow fever epidemic, settled in this district after 1871 showing their love for the French École de Baux Arts. The Círculo Militar, which used to be the house of the Paz family, the owner of an important newspaper called La Prensa; the Chancellery, which used to be the residence of the Anchorena family; the building that houses the headquarters of Parques Nacionales (National Parks), the former house of the Haedo family, are all beautiful examples of that French style.

The 120 metre high Kavanagh building was for many years the highest building made of reinforced concrete in the world.

Monument to San Martín.
This sculpture by L.J. Daumas was designed after the model of the statue of Louis xiv in Paris. It is the first equestrian statue in Buenos Aires.
The reliefs were made by G. Eberlein and they represent San Martín's battles and the Andes Campain.

Entrance to the Paz Palace, today the Círculo Militar.

The church Santisimo Sacramento was donated by Mercedes Castellanos de Anchorena at the beginning of the twentieth century.

Plaza Hotel.
This hotel, built in 1909, belongs to the Marriot Chain and it is the most famous hotel in Buenos Aires. It has received many famous guests: the Maharaja of Kapurtala, Farah Diba, Charles De Gaulle, Charles Chaplin, Luciano Pavarotti, Errol Flynn, Gina Lollobrigida, María Félix, Arturo Toscanini, Indira Gandhi, Theodore Roosevelt, the King of Belgium, Phillip of Edimbourg, Prince Al Faisal, and many others.

The houses at this residential district around San Martín Square also show the French style copied in Buenos Aires: the Estrougamou Building (1926), the Bencich Building, refurbished as a beautiful Sofitel Hotel are good examples of this tendency.

In turn, some families copied the Spanish colonial style. That was the case of architect Martín Noel who built his house at Suipacha street. Today it has become a museum which houses a very important collection of Southamerican colonial art.

The Jockey Club of Buenos Aires at Carlos Pellegrini Square. In the hall, a beautiful Diana by A. Falguière.

The Palacio Pereda is today the Embassy of Brazil. Its ceilings have been painted by José María Sert.

The Palacio Ortíz Basualdo is today the French Embassy. It was designed by the architect Pablo Pater in 1913. (p. 85)

RECOLETA

The monastery of the Franciscan Fathers had been built in 1716, and in 1732, the church of Nuestra Señora del Pilar was inaugurated. The church was designed by Andrés Bianchi and Juan Bautista Premolí, two Jesuits who were responsible for many churches in Buenos Aires. The Pilar is one of the few temples in Buenos Aires which still has its original façade. The altar is a superb work of an Indian artist, its altar frontal is made of Peruvian silverwork.

When the Franciscan Congregation was forced to leave in 1821, the vegetable garden of the brethren was turned into a cemetery and the monastery into an asylum for poor people.

In the 1980ies the old asylum was transformed into an art gallery and a design centre.

San Martín de Tours is the Patron Saint
of the city of Buenos Aires.

Church of Nuestra Señora del Pilar.
It houses old works of art, sculptures, altars, relics, and its magnificent altar.
It is one of the best examples of colonial art in Buenos Aires.
(p. 89)

90

The Cemetery of the Recoleta has given its name to the whole district. Many people who have been important in Argentine history are buried in this cemetery, which is visited by many tourists when they come to Buenos Aires.

Even at the time of the Franciscan Monastery there were fairs held in front of the church.

The huge *Ficus macrophylia* in front of the square, which is more than two hundred years old, has been the privileged witness of all those meetings.

Nowadays, the square is the hub of part of the cultural, artistic and commercial life of Buenos Aires. There are also very well known restaurants and cafés where the porteños meet to eat.

The Cultural Centre Recoleta was refurbished in 1980. It is a good example of the style brought by the Jesuits such as Juan Krauss and Juan Wolff.

Recoleta Cemetery.

This old building has been refurbished as a fashionable shopping centre.

La Biela. Traditional café in Recoleta.

The cemetery marked the limit of the city, beyond the cemetery there were stockyards, the slaughterhouse and the route to the North. The neighbourhood was full of workers and bars. It was the perfect scenery for the tango. The tango may well have been born here.

Today this is the most elegant district of the city with its buildings of the end of the nineteenth century, its posh hotels and shops. The Alvear Palace Hotel on Avenida Alvear with its beautiful shops and galleries, was designed during the government of Torcuato the Alvear in 1885. In 1869 a tramway line linked the district with the Plaza de Mayo.

The Avenida Quintana was called the Calle Larga, the Long Street, in the eighteenth century. Here again are famous shops.

Alvear Palace Hotel.
It has had famous guests such as the Prince of Wales, María Callas, Arthur Miller, Sharon Stone, Helmuth Kohl, the King of Spain, Nelson Mandela, Sofía Loren, Magic Johnson and Michael Schumacher.

The National Museum of Art uses the house where the pumps for the water provision of Buenos Aires were placed. The museum has a very important art collection, statues and pictures, not only by foreign artists, but also American and Argentine.

The monument to General Carlos María de Alvear by the French sculptor A. Bourdelle is the best equestrian monument in Buenos Aires.

Intendente Alvear Square. (p. 95)

The building of the Law Faculty was finished in 1944.

Floralis Genérica.
This moving sculpture was donated and inaugu-rated by Eduardo Catalano in April 2002.

PALERMO

In 1590 this plot of land was bought by an Italian called Giovanni Doménico Palermo who cultivated vines and fruits in what is today the biggest park of Buenos Aires. Since then, the district has been called Palermo. At the beginning of the nineteenth century the plot of land was bought by Juan Manuel de Rosas, who built his residence in the corner of Sarmiento and del Libertador Avenues.

The place was then called San Benito de Palermo and it became the residence of a politician who governed the country with firm hand and strong discipline from 1828 to 1852. The land filled with earth from a hill nearby, was turned into a park and a private zoo with native animals.

After the battle of Caseros, in 1852, when Rosas was overthrown, the villa was taken by General J.J. de Urquiza, the general who led the victorious army.

The Planetary Galileo Galilei.
This planetary with a dome of twenty metres in diameter, is the biggest one in Argentina.

The first sports activities in Argentina were started in a club nearby. It was called Buenos Aires Cricket Club and had been organized by English residents.

The club was inaugurated with a cricket match played by the team of the Cricket Club and the team formed by the crew of an English ship. In 1867, the first football match was played and the first athletics competition took place in 1878. The first rugby match was in 1873 and tennis was started in 1886.

President Domingo Faustino Sarmiento decided to create the Tres de Febrero Park, the date of the Battle of Caceros. The French architect Charles Thays was commissioned to design the park.

Originally, the park had 400 hectares, today it has only 25. The rest was transformed into a Botanical Garden, a Zoo, golf places, an exhibition centre for the Rural Society, sports clubs, a hippodrome, polo fields, an airport and even an Islamic centre with the biggest Mesquite in South America.

The Botanical Garden in almost eight hectares has around 5000 trees, bushes and plants, not only native plants, but exotic ones as well. It was inaugurated in 1898 and it was again designed by Charles Thays.

The big glasshouse in the Botanical Garden.

The Zoo.
The zoo was built on an 18 hectare big plot of land. It has some exotic constructions that house the animals according to their origin. There is a Japanese pagoda, a temple from Hindustan, an Arabic house, an Egyptian temple, Greek ruins. The elephants live in the copy of a palace of the goddess Nimashi in Bombay, dedicated to Shiva. The two first directors of the zoo Eduardo Holmberg and Clemente Onelli, were responsible for these constructions.

The monument to Domingo F. Sarmiento was made by A. Rodin and it was placed where Rosas house used to be. He was his fiercest enemy.

The Japanese Garden.
This oriental park was presented to
Buenos Aires by the Japanese Society
in Argentina.

To enter the Rosedal one has to cross the bridge.

Red Riding Hood.
The sculpture by Jean Carlus, is placed
in Sicily Square in Palermo.

To the north and west of Palermo, there are residential districts, which are called Palermo Chico, Small Palermo; Palermo Viejo, Old Palermo, and Palermo Hollywood.

Palermo Chico, also called Barrio Parque is probably the most elegant residential district in Buenos Aires with its French residences, many of which are embassies today.

Palermo Viejo, also called Villa Alvear, with its refurbished old houses is now the neighbourhood of bohemian people.

In Palermo Hollywood, the newest of the three, there are many television studios and modern restaurants.

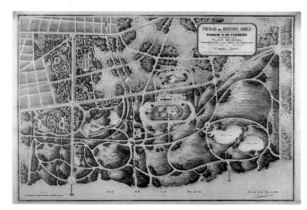

Design by Charles Thays for Palermo Park.

*A blooming lapacho
in Palermo Chico.*

Spanish Monument.
This monument called Magna Charta represents
the four regions of Argentina and was a present
of Spanish residents in Argentina. It was
inaugurated in 1927.

Palermo is the park used by many porteños to spend their weekends in the open air.

To the east of Palermo, the Costanera Avenue, a promenade along the coast of the river, is the place where fishermen meet. In very clear days one can see the Uruguayan coast.

110

A blooming Jacarandá (Jacarandá mimosifolia) in Palermo.
Buenos Aires gets a lavender blue carpet every November.

Pato is a sport similar to polo and basketball. One needs courage and hability to play it.
(Photograph, Carlos María Bazán)

In Buenos Aires, in spring, one can see the best polo in the world. The Campo Argentino de Polo in Palermo, is the main polo field.
(Photograph, Carlos María Bazán)

Islamic Cultural Centre King Fahd.
This mesquite,the biggest in South America, can
receive up to 1600 people. It was designed by the
Arabic architect Zuhair Fayez.

In the 150 metre long fishermen's
pier is the Fishermen's Club
which was built in 1937.

San Isidro

San Isidro, a residential district, is twenty kilometres away from the centre of Buenos Aires. In colonial times, the rich inhabitants of Buenos Aires built their villas there. San Martín thought and organized his campaign in San Isidro in the old villa built by his friend Juan Martín de Pueyrredón. From this villa, which houses a museum, one gets o very good view of the Río de la Plata.

There are very good golf courses in San Isidro and there is also a very big hippodrome which belongs to the most famous club in Argentina: the Jockey Club.

Pueyrredon´s Villa
In this villa, the famous painter Prilidiano Pueyrredón used to paint the neighbourhood of San Isidro.

Jockey Club in San Isidro.

Pueyrredon´s Villa

San Isidro Cathedral.
This neo gothic Cathedral is in the very centre
of the district. A relic of the Patron Saint of Ma-
drid, San Isidro, was presented to this Cathedral
by the people of Madrid.

Tigre Hotel.

Club de Regatas La Marina.

Tigre

The delta, only 32 kilometres away from Buenos Aires, connects two very big rivers: the Paraná River and the Uruguay River, which together flow into the Río de la Plata.

The formation of the delta started 6000 years ago by the accumulation of sediments brought by the Paraná River and today the delta is more than 300 kilometres long. It grows about 50 to 90 metres a year.

It is from 50 to 100 kilometres wide and it is made up of many small rivers. The climate is similar to the subtropical climate of the source of the Paraná, and the subtropical vegetation is a result of it.

After the Spanish colonization, the islands were occupied by Jesuit missionaries who taught the natives to cultivate the soil.

When the Jesuits were forced to leave the country, the delta fell into the hands of privateers, corsairs and smugglers. The place was also inhabited by political refugees, who found that the delta was an easy place to hide in.

By the end of the nineteenth century, a law was passed and the islands were sold to many European immigrants who started working on the islands.

There is a very strong contrast between the frantic life of the city of Buenos Aires and the tranquillity of the islands of the delta in Tigre.

Rowing Club.

*Yaguareté,
American tiger
(Leo onca).*

The vegetation smells of orange blossom and eucalyptus and the trees border the banks of the rivulets. High above the jungle, the pindó palm tree *(Arecastrum romanzoffianum)* can be seen from far away. Part of the delta is called the Paraná de las Palmas, the Paraná of the Palm Trees. In spring time the seibos *(Erythrina crista–galli)* are in full bloom. Their red flower is Argentina's national flower.

There is a great variety of birds: coots, herons, humming birds and colourful scarlet headed blackbirds.

The scenery is completed by big ships that carry all sorts of cargo, by sportsmen who practice all kinds of water sports and by patient fishermen.

The best way to get to the delta is by the station of Tigre (which means tiger, because apparently there were many *yaguaretés* in the region, the *yaguareté (Leo onca)* is the American tiger). The neighbourhood of Tigre was a beloved district between the end of the nineteenth century and the beginning of the twentieth century. Many families had their villas in Tigre and in summer there were many parties and fairs which were held at the luxury hotels and elegant houses and clubs.

In 1873, the first official regatta took place.

New Railway Station in Tigre.

LUJÁN

The city of Luján is 68 kilometres away from Buenos Aires. It is the sanctuary of the Virgen de Luján, the Virgin of Luján, Patroness of Argentina. Every year more than six million people go to Luján to pay a visit to the Virgin.

Captain Don Diego de Luján, who arrived with Pedro de Mendoza, was killed by the Querandí Indians in 1536 near a river which has been called Luján ever since.

A hundred years later, in 1630, thanks to the miracle of the Virgin, Luján started growing. In the middle of the eighteenth century, the Cabildo was created and a colonial style church was constructed.

The city has been the witness if important happenings during the history of Agentina, especially during the English Invasions in 1806 and 1807.

Today Luján has over 80.000 inhabitants but still leads the life of a small city full of austerity and generosity.

It was visited twice by Pope Johannes Paulus II, in 1982 and in 1987.

"Luján Basilica" W. Dohme.
The Luján Basilica, built in French gothic style, was finished in 1935. It is 97 metres long and the towers are 106,05 metres high. The towers end in a 6 meter long cross.

The Townhall (Cabildo) and the Museum in Luján.
The Museum in Luján is worth visiting. Here one can get a very good idea of what life used to be in Argentina 200 years ago.

"The Rodeo", P. Pueyrredón (1823–1870).

THE PAMPAS

The *pampa* is the endless plain in Argentina. Today that immense territory has been divided into estancias (farms) which produce large amounts of corn and where cattle raising is also one of the principal activities.

The two characters responsible for these activities were the *estanciero*, the owner of the farm, and the *gaucho*, the native herdsman.

Today one can visit those big farm houses, where the *estancieros* lived as if they had lived in Paris or in London. Everything needed for the building of these estancias, was brought from Europe and today many of these beautiful mansions have been transformed into hotels. They are very well furnished, better than the best hotels. Some of them are in French or English style, others in Spanish colonial style.

In these estancias, the guests can take part in all rural activities: rodeos, cattle marking, milking and the breaking in of horses. One can ride out to watch the flora and fauna of the place.

The principal dish is going to be the *asado*, meat on the barbecue with the best Argentine wines.

Estancia Santa Susana.

Estancia Santa Susana.

Estancia Santa Susana.

Estancia Santa Susana.

The *gaucho* used to be the nomadic horseman of the Pampas. Today he stands as the embodiment of loyalty and freedom and has become the *paisano*, the rural labourer.

The foreign travellers, especially those who came to Argentina in the nineteenth century, looked at the gauchos in fascination. An English traveller T.W. Hinchliff, wrote about the *gauchos*: "Most of them do a hard work very steadily without food till the evening announces the time of their rest; they loll or sit lazily about the fire where their beef is cooking, while the inevitable cigarette ornaments their sunburnt faces; and if I may judge by my own experience, I should say they pass their evening remarkably quietly in their own quartier of the estancia; where they peaceably gorge themselves with meat and mate".

"The Two Paths", J. M. Blanes (1830–1901).

Index

Buenos Aires is an important milestone in the history of Art Nouveau in the world. Most of the buildings constructed in this style may be found in the neighbourhoods of Montserrat, Congreso and Once. They were used not only as private houses but they were used as cinemas, theatres and hotels as well.